From the Farm to the Table
Dairy

by

Kathy Coatney

CONTENTS

Dedication

To Farmer John, the cow guy whose dedication to his animals is an inspiration.

Acknowledgements

Many thanks to those who have assisted me with this project. Georgia Bockoven, who put the idea in my head. Thanks to Dr. Mike Karle, DVM, for his time and expertise. Patti Thurman, and Jenny Reilly, who consulted and proofread for me. To my email check-in pals, Jennifer Skullestad and Lisa Sorensen, a huge thanks. Luann Erickson, Susan Crosby, Karol Black, and Tammy Lambeth, who critiqued and supported me through the process. To the Redding Lunch Bunch, Libby, Shari, Dianna, Lisa, Terry, and Patti, you're the best. To my family, Nick, Wade and Devin, Collin and Ellis, Jake and Emily, Allie and Russell. You all have been my inspiration. Thank you. I never would have made it without you.

Note to parents and teachers: The words in bold are second-grade vocabulary words. A list of the words used can be found at the end of the book.

Also By

Thank you for reading **From the Farm to the Table Dairy**, book 1 in **From the Farm to the Table series** of picture books.

I love hearing from my fans. You can contact me through my website: www.kathycoatney.com.

From the Farm to the Table

From the Farm to the Table Dairy
From the Farm to the Table Bees
From the Farm to the Table Olives
From the Farm to the Table Potatoes
From the Farm to the Table Almonds
From the Farm to the Table Beef

Stand Alone Picture Book
Dad's Girls

From the Farm to the Table Dairy

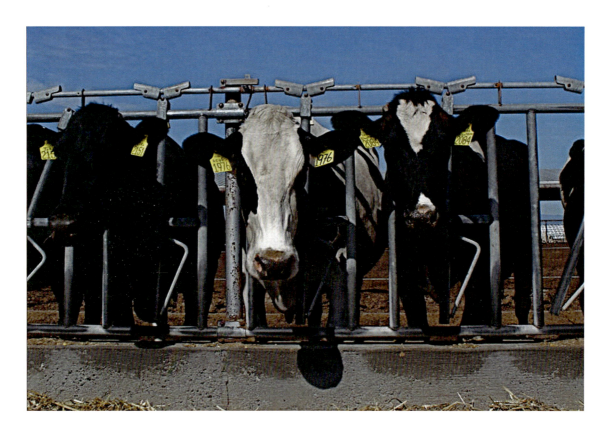

Farmer John is a cow guy. Even before he was old enough to go to school, he loved cows, <u>especially</u> dairy cows. He liked their shape. He liked their black, black eyes, and he loved that
they gave him sweet, lip-smacking milk.

Milk made Farmer John other things he loved, like cheese and yogurt and butter and buttermilk, which gave more things he loved. Like pancakes and bread. Milk even made special, special treats like ice cream that he loved on a hot summer day.

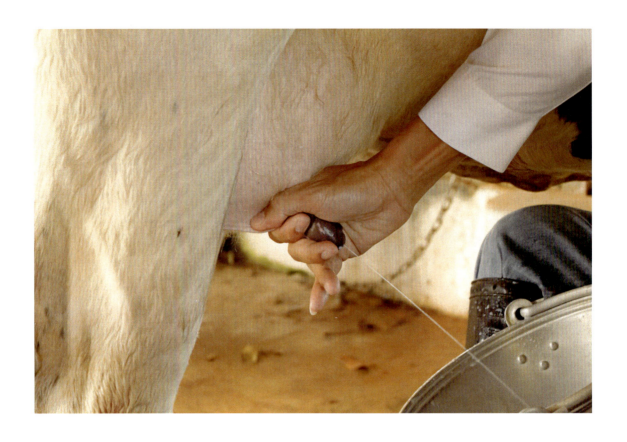

Farmer John grew up on a dairy farm in California that his daddy, Farmer Lawrence, started in 1900, more than 100 years ago. When Farmer John turned six, he was given a new <u>chore</u>.

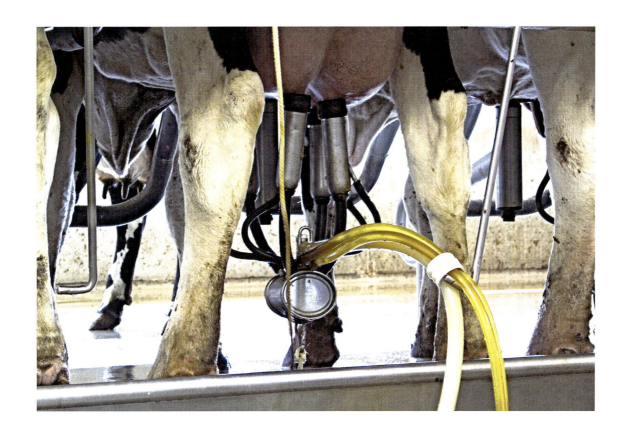

Farmer John started milking cows. Cows were milked by hand back then. Now there are machines that milk the cows.

Farmer John grew and grew and grew, and when he finished school he kept working on his daddy's dairy. He worked hard and he loved it.

Farmer John spent his days and a lot of nights with cows. He milked them, he fed them, he took care of them when they were sick, and he watched over them when they had their calves. Baby cows are called calves.

More years went by and Farmer John got married and started his own family. He worked on the dairy, and he also started a processing plant. A processing plant is where milk is pasteurized and put into bottles. Milk is pasteurized by cooking it.

Farmer John's drive-in milk store

After the milk was in the bottles, Farmer John sold it, along with butter and eggs, in a drive-in milk store. He also sold his milk to schools and hospitals and stores. One day he moved his family and the dairy to northern California.

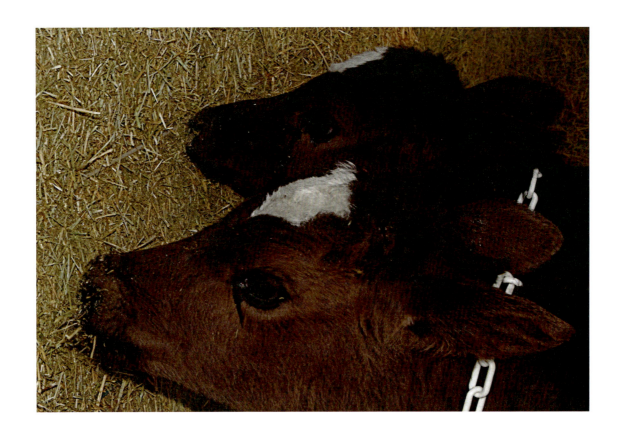

Farmer John's cows each have one calf every year, but occasionally a cow will have two calves. When a cow has two calves they are called twins. That happens once every 96 times cows have calves.

Sometimes cows have three calves, called triplets, and that happens once every 7,500 times cows have calves. And sometimes a miracle happens and cows have four calves, called quadruplets. That happens once every 700,000 times cows have calves.

Over 70 years passed, and
Farmer John's cows had many,
many, many calves. Then one
day, Farmer John had a very
special cow.

This cow was so special, in fact, all ten of his grandchildren came up with a name for her. They called her Ten Gallon Maybelle because she always gave ten gallons of milk every day.

From each gallon Maybelle
produced, Farmer John received
128 ounces of milk, and 128
ounces equals 16 8–ounce glasses
of milk. So for every gallon of milk
Maybelle made, Farmer John got
16 glasses of milk, more than
enough milk to <u>satisfy</u> his thirst.

Ten gallons of milk gave Farmer John 160 glasses of milk every day. That was enough to feed fifty–three people three glasses a day! And Farmer John says that's important because milk is really, really good for you to drink.

Maybelle was a black–and–white Holstein cow. When she was four years old she got pregnant. Dr. Mike, Farmer John's veterinarian, a doctor who takes care of animals, <u>examined</u> Maybelle and did a test called an ultrasound. The ultrasound takes pictures of the calf inside the cow.

Dr. Mike <u>inspected</u> the ultrasound picture, but only two calves appeared in the picture–twins. What no one–not even Maybelle–<u>realized</u> was there were two more calves, which meant she was carrying quadruplets. Farmer John didn't know it, but he was about to witness a miracle.

Maybelle was given extra special care because cows that are pregnant with more than one calf need more food than cows that have one calf.

Cows need really, really good nutrition when they are pregnant. In fact, cows need to eat a perfect balance of high quality feed every day to stay healthy and nourish themselves, and satisfy the calf's nutritional needs. They also need to eat really, really well to produce lots of sweet, creamy milk after the calf is born.

Maybelle's gestation period, how long she is pregnant, is close to what human mommies have, about 285 days or nine–and–a–half months. So, about nine–and–a–half months later, Maybelle went into labor in a special pen set aside for her.

Farmer John checked on her, and she had two heifer calves. Heifers are girl calves that haven't had babies yet.

Farmer John came back a little while later and found two more heifer calves. When he saw all four calves <u>nestled</u> together, he called them his Four Quart Girls because they reminded him four quarts make a gallon.

Farmer John had a smile as wide as the Sacramento River that flowed past his farm. Never in all his years had anything this <u>incredible</u> happened to him.

Not only had Maybelle been pregnant with quadruplets, but she gave birth to them without any help from Dr. Mike, and they were all healthy and happy. That only happens once every 11.2 million births. But even more <u>amazing</u> was they were all heifer calves.

For Maybelle to have quadruplets, without assistance, all healthy and happy and heifer calves only happens once in every 179.2 million births. That's more than all the leaves in the big, big oak tree that shades Farmer John's house.

Because this was such a special event, Dr. Mike had a special test done called deoxyribonucleic (de•oxy•ri•bo•nu•cle•ic) acid, DNA for short. The test discovered that two of the calves were from the same egg, and the other two calves each had their own egg.

    Calves from the same egg are called identical twins. Calves that have their own eggs are called fraternal twins.

One calf usually weighs 85 pounds when it is born, but Maybelle had quadruplets, and they weighed 65 pounds each. That means Maybelle had to feed 260 more pounds besides herself. That is a lot of work!

Maybelle was really, really tired after the calves were born, so Farmer John fed her the very best food he had. Now she is healthy and making lots and lots of delicious milk.

Because Maybelle was so special, Farmer John carved a statue of her and Farmer Lawrence, his daddy, and the quadruplets out of walnut wood, his very favorite wood. They stand at the entrance to Farmer John's dairy.

Now, every time Farmer John drives past the carving, he remembers Ten Gallon Maybelle was the cow that not only gave him ten gallons of milk every day, but she also gave him the Four Quart Girls. Together they made a very special gallon.

The End

Vocabulary List

Amazing
Chore
Especially
Examined
Incredible
Inspected
Nestled
Realized
Satisfy

Author Biography

Kathy Coatney has worked as a freelance photojournalist for 35 years, starting in parenting magazines, then fly fishing, and finally specializing in agriculture. Her work can be seen in the California Farm Bureau magazine, Ag Alert and West Coast Nut magazine.

Visit her website at: www.KathyCoatney.com

Made in United States
North Haven, CT
22 February 2025

66168070R00024